CORN
in the story of agriculture

Susan Anderson & JoAnne Buggey

Book design by Nancy Roberts

Northwest Arm Press

Hello!

I'm Agri-Culture, Agri for short.

I'm here to introduce **corn,** an important agricultural product.

We will see corn in all five parts of agriculture:

production 〉 processing 〉 distribution 〉 marketing 〉 consumerism 〉

Let's go!

Chapter 1 • The production of corn

Agricultural production is growing crops or raising animals.

| production | processing | distribution | marketing | consumerism |

- seeds and plants
- farming
- harvesting and storage
- sweet corn and popcorn

Corn has likely been grown in Mexico for over 5,000 years. Another word for corn, maize, comes from a Native Caribbean language. Columbus reportedly took corn back to Spain.

Did you know?

The Sacagawea dollar commemorates Native American corn agriculture. Native Americans taught the first English colonists in northeastern North America how to plant corn. It helped them survive their first winters here.

silks

husks

It's a fact!

This is an ear of field, or dent, corn. Almost all of the corn grown in the United States is field corn.

Kernels cover each ear of corn. Look at the picture of a kernel of field, or dent, corn. Can you see the dent? The kernel is also the seed.

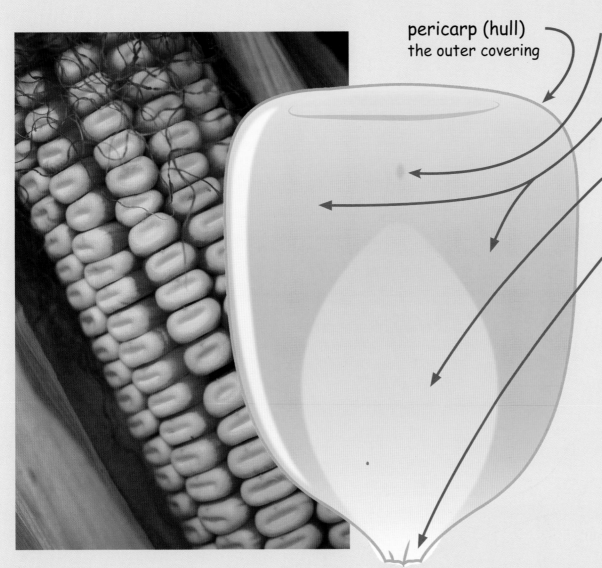

pericarp (hull)
the outer covering

silk scar
where the silk was attached; hard to see, but you might feel it

endosperm
starch and fiber filling the inside

germ
the part that could grow into a new corn plant

tip cap
where the kernel takes in water and nutrients from the plant

It's a fact!
Each ear of corn has about 800 kernels and an even number of rows.

Did you know?
Some other kinds of corn are sweet corn and popcorn.

These are corn **plants.** One seed is needed to grow each plant.

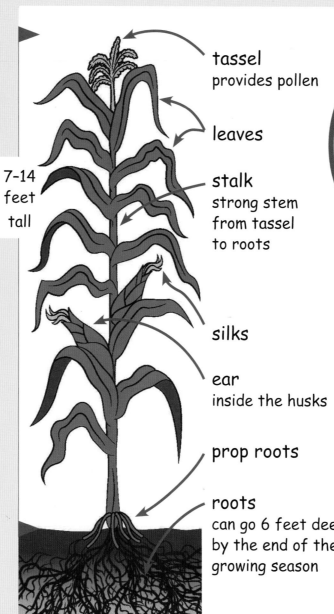

7–14 feet tall

tassel
provides pollen

leaves

stalk
strong stem from tassel to roots

silks

ear
inside the husks

prop roots

roots
can go 6 feet deep by the end of the growing season

It's a fact!

The pollen from the tassels must fall on the silks to produce the kernels. Each silk leads the pollen to where a kernel will form on the ear.

Did you know?

A stalk usually produces one or two good ears of corn.

It is **spring.** Corn is being planted in this field.

It's a fact!

This machine is a planter. Rows are planted 20 to 30 inches apart. Approximately 30,000 seeds are planted per acre, which is about the size of a football field. Planters come in different sizes – this one plants eight rows at a time.

Did you know?

Corn farmers work all year long.

Spring
- Prepare the soil
- Plant seeds

Summer
- Control weeds
- Control insects
- Irrigate where necessary

Fall
- Harvest
- Store corn
- Work the soil

Winter
- Market the crop
- Order seeds
- Take care of machinery

Summer has come. The field corn is growing rapidly.

Did you know?

Weather is very important to corn producers. If there is not enough rainfall to grow a good corn crop, some farmers use irrigation to provide water.

It's a fact!

Ninety percent of all the corn grown is produced by family farms.

Now it is **fall.** A combine harvests field corn. It pulls the ears from the stalks, separates the husks from the ears, and removes the kernels from the cobs. When the combine's tank is full of kernels, the combine pours them into a truck or cart.

Did you know?

It takes about 90 to 120 days for field corn to mature. The stalks, leaves, and ears of corn stop growing and become dry and golden brown.

It's a fact!

Corn yields are measured in bushels per acre. Yields per acre have gone from about 25 bushels in the 1930s to around 150 today. A bushel of corn weighs close to 56 pounds and contains approximately 72,000 kernels.

Sweet corn is harvested as whole ears by a corn picking machine.

Did you know?

Some sweet corn is harvested by hand and sold fresh for corn on the cob. However, most sweet corn is processed into frozen or canned products so it can be enjoyed year-round.

It's a fact!

Sweet corn is picked when the kernels are still soft and juicy. At that point the corn is especially sweet. It can be yellow, white, or a combination called bicolor.

Have you ever eaten **popcorn?** The ears of corn shown here are popcorn.

It's a fact!

Popcorn is the only corn that pops. It has the thickest pericarp (hull) of any corn. This makes the kernel very strong, so steam pressure can build up inside the kernel to the point of popping.

Did you know?

Popcorn is usually eaten as a snack. It is a common movie treat.

Back to field corn. These trucks are delivering field corn from the farm to nearby storage areas called **elevators.**

Did you know?

The United States is the leading producer of field corn. It grows two of every five of the world's bushels of corn.

It's a fact!

Corn is a renewable resource. That means we won't run out because farmers can grow a new crop every year.

Chapter 2 • The **processing** of corn

Processing is making crops or animals into products you can eat or use.

production | **processing** | distribution | marketing | consumerism

- animal feed
- cereals and sweeteners
- ethanol
- cloth and plastic
- sweet corn

Animal feed is the biggest single use of field corn.

Did you know?

Corn becomes animal feed in more than one way. Corn kernels can be cracked or ground and mixed with other grains and nutrients. This is the main way corn is made into feed.

It's a fact!

Corn is found in many pet foods. Check your pet's food to see if it contains some form of corn.

Field corn can also be **processed** into a variety of different products we eat, including cereals and sweeteners.

It's a fact!

Will Keith Kellogg and his brother Dr. John Harvey Kellogg discovered the process for making corn flakes in 1894. This eventually led to the Kellogg's cereal company we know today.

Did you know?

Field corn's biggest use in foods and drinks is as a sweetener – high fructose or corn syrup. The sweeteners are made from the starch in the kernel.

Ethanol is a biofuel manufactured from field corn in refineries like this one.

Did you know?

Refineries produce 2.8 gallons of ethanol from one bushel of field corn, using only the starch. The remaining nutrients – protein, fiber, and germ – are used in livestock feed.

It's a fact!

Today's flex-fuel vehicles (FFVs) are designed to run on E85, a blended fuel that is 85 percent ethanol. Most major car-makers now offer FFV vehicles.

Corn is found almost everywhere. Even **cloth and plastic** can be made from the starch in field corn.

It's a fact!

Nonfood products like plastic containers and fibers for clothes, blankets, pillows, and yarn are one of corn's fastest-growing markets.

Did you know?

Many sports events are using forks, straws, and drink cups made from corn.

Sweet corn can be processed for canning or freezing. This helps to keep it fresh for a longer period of time.

Did you know?

Less than one percent of the corn grown by corn producers is sweet corn, yet sweet corn is the type of corn most of us know best. It's the corn we eat as a vegetable, either on the cob or as niblets.

It's a fact!

Corn is easily digestible and provides high-quality carbohydrates for energy.

Chapter 3 • The **distribution** of corn

Distribution is delivering a product from where it is produced or grown to the places where it will be used.

production	processing	**distribution**	marketing	consumerism

- corn-producing states
- corn exports
- transportation

Corn is grown throughout the United States.

It's a fact!

In the United States most corn is grown in the states shown in color. The area where most of the corn is grown is often called the Corn Belt.

Did you know?

The top five corn-producing states are Illinois, Indiana, Iowa, Minnesota, and Nebraska, Together these states grow over 50 percent of the corn. Do you live in one of the major corn-producing states?

Field corn is a leading **export** of the United States.

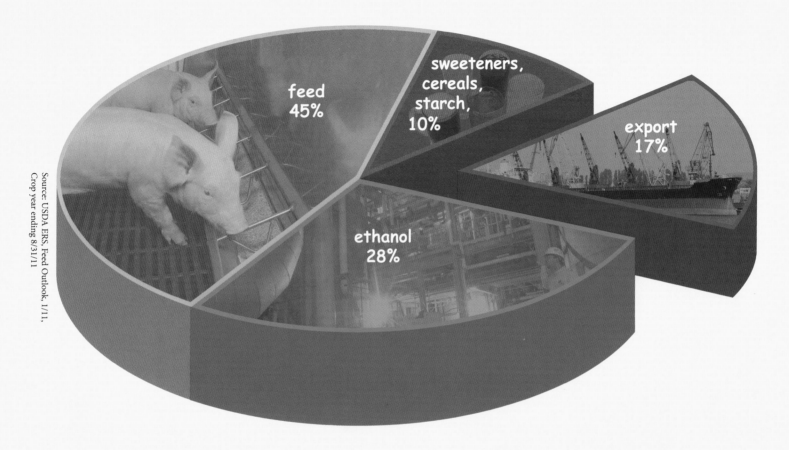

feed
45%

sweeteners,
cereals,
starch,
10%

export
17%

ethanol
28%

Source: USDA ERS, Feed Outlook, 1/11,
Crop year ending 8/31/11

It's a fact!

The United States exports a significant amount of its corn production. The five top destinations are Japan, Mexico, South Korea, Taiwan, and Egypt.

Did you know?

Corn is an important ingredient in animal feed. When we export beef, pork, and poultry, this is an indirect way of exporting corn.

Distributing corn from growing areas requires a good **transportation** system.

Did you know?

The corn used within the United States moves by truck, rail, and river barge.

It's a fact!

Most of the export corn travels on barges down the Mississippi River to New Orleans. The Port of New Orleans is important for the export of corn.

Chapter 4 • The marketing of corn

Marketing is telling about products so that you will know about them and might buy them.

| production | processing | distribution | marketing | consumerism |

- buildings and monuments
- popularity
- logos

We **celebrate** and learn about corn in many different ways.

Did you know?

Olivia, Minnesota, calls itself the Corn Capital of the World and has this rooftop ornament to prove it.

The Corn Palace of Mitchell, South Dakota, was built in 1892 to advertise the products of local farmers. Its murals and decorations are made of corn and other grains and grasses. They are removed and changed each year.

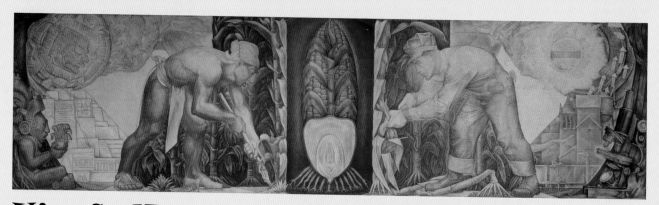

It's a fact! Inside the Ames, Iowa, post office is this 18-foot mural showing ancient and modern corn farming. It was created in 1936–38 by Lowell Houser.

Corn has been **important** for a long time. We see it in many places besides food.

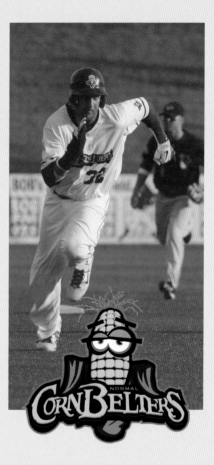

Did you know?

Some people collect corn memorabilia because they either grow corn or like to eat corn – or just like the way it looks.

It's a fact!

One way to make corn popular is to connect it to other things people enjoy. An example is the CornBelters baseball team in Normal, Illinois.

These are some **logos** for corn products and organizations.

Did you know?

One way to advertise is to develop a logo to identify a product. Look to see if there is a corn organization in your state. Does it have corn in its logo?

Illinois Corn Marketing Board

It's a fact!

Through Future Farmers of America (FFA) and 4-H, young people can share information about corn. The FFA in Clarke County, Kentucky, mowed the FFA logo into a cornfield to make a recreational corn maze!

Chapter 5 • **Consumerism** and corn

Consumerism is **you** choosing, buying, and using products.

production | processing | distribution | marketing | **consumerism**

- MyPlate
- corn foods
- the future

Corn is included in the **Grains** or **Vegetables** food group, depending on how it is prepared.

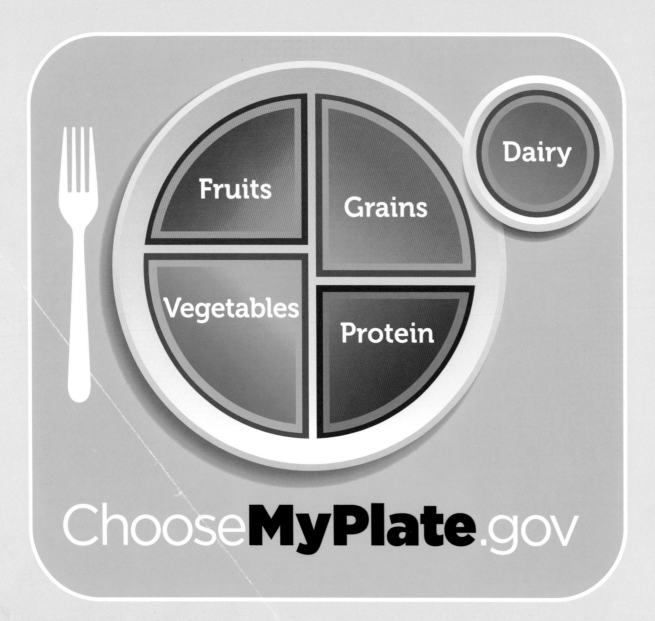

Fruits

Grains

Dairy

Vegetables

Protein

Choose**MyPlate**.gov

It's a fact!

Corn eaten as creamed corn, niblets, and corn on the cob or in soup, succotash, or shepherd's pie counts as a vegetable. Corn in hot and cold cereals and breads counts as a grain.

Did you know?

You can find foods that contain corn in almost every aisle of the grocery store.

These are some of the ways we **eat** corn. Point to the ones you have eaten.

Did you know?

Cornmeal is made from ground-up field corn. It can be used for corn bread, tamales, tortillas, and chips.

It's a fact!

Corn might be eaten at every meal.

There is enough corn for all our **future** needs – feed, food, fiber, and fuel.

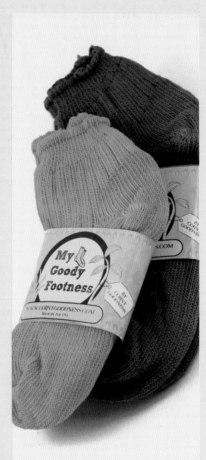

Corn is an important part of our lives. Maybe **you** will play a role in the future of corn.

Corn Activities

- Write your own story about each chapter.

- Divide a page of paper into four parts and draw a picture in each part, showing something you learned about corn.

- Look at your school lunches for corn products.

- Make a list of all the ways you can eat corn.

- Make an A-to-Z list about corn.

- Make a list of cereals that have corn named as the first ingredient.

- Work with an adult to prepare fresh corn three different ways. Which way did you like best?

- Make a list of corn snacks.

- Look at several ears of corn. Count the rows. What did you find? Compare your findings with others'. What surprised you?

Popcorn Balls *Fun and easy!*

Ingredients:
16 cups (6-ounce bag) of popped popcorn
6 tablespoons of butter
5 cups (10.5-ounce bag) of miniature marshmallows

Directions: (*Cook with an adult.*)
1. Grease a large bowl, empty popcorn into it, set aside.
2. Melt butter in medium-sized saucepan over low heat.
3. Add marshmallows, stirring constantly until melted.
4. Pour the heated mixture into the popcorn.
5. Mix with spatula or spoon until the popcorn is evenly coated.
6. Allow the mixture to cool slightly to protect your hands.
7. Grease your hands.
8. Shape the mixture firmly into balls.

Makes about 8 balls.